I0571736

VENOM & GRACE
A HOLY REBELLION

Ruth-Ann Walker

Copyright © 2026 by Ruth-Ann Walker

All rights reserved.

No part of this book may be reproduced in any form or by any electronic or mechanical means, including information storage and retrieval systems, without written permission from the author, except for the use of brief quotations in a book review.

Venom & Grace *First Edition: 2026*

ISBN: 979-8-9992848-3-9

Published by: Ruth-Ann Walker

Printed in the United States of America

"We began with God, and it's God till the end.
If I am ever anything, let it go to Calvary."

For the girl who survived.

They want me softer, smaller, silent?
Too bad.
I won't shrink just to be digestible.
Let 'em choke on every ounce
of the woman they swore I'd never become.

THE KINGDOM OF ASH 8

HELL CAT..9

LOVE MADE A LIAR 11

WHY DO YOU HATE ME SO? 12

WHY DO I CHASE YOU? 16

DON'T BE SO FAMILIAR WITH HEARTBREAK
....18

THE SAME WORDS...................................20

THE PAST...21

TOO MUCH FOR YOU TO SWALLOW 24

SIMMERING...26

LET THE BRIDGES BURN 29

ACCESS REVOKED 31

THE LOUDEST SILENCE 32

FROM EGYPT TO MANNA 33

OFF THE MAP..35

UNBILLED JOURNEYS 37

NOT ON THE GUEST LIST 38

TIGHT SCHEDULE....................................39

WHEN WE ARE DOWN TO NOTHING.............41

ETCHED IN SILENCE................................43

I WISH I COULD TELL YOU.....................44

DON'T LET GO...46

I DIDN'T FORCE HEAVEN 49

IT'S ALREADY LATE 50

TIME IS TICKING 51

THE HOLY INTRUSION 54

WHEN I KNEEL 55

CONVERSATION AT THE ALTAR 58

THE ALTAR I BUILT 60

WHEN I FINALLY SEE 63

THE SHAKING 65

WHEN THE KING CALLS 66

WHERE LOGIC KNEELS 69

THE ROD AND THE STAFF 71

THE WEAPON 72

WHO AM I TO CHANGE YOUR MIND 74

THE POTTER'S HANDS 75

HE KNOWS WHAT I CANNOT SEE 77

THE SABOTAGE 79

GOD KEEPS RECORDS 81

NOT LIKE MAN 82

THE KEEPER OF THE KEYS 84

THE PROLIFIC SUSPENSE WRITER 87

THE HEAVY CROWN 89

WHEN GOD ARISES 90

ROUSE THE ANCIENT OF DAYS 92

THE OVERFLOWING SEASON 95

DRIPPING IN FAVOR 97

NO CO-SIGNERS 99

DECREE OF THE TABLE 101

THE MARK OF THE KING 103

UNTOUCHABLE IN GOD 106

ASHES AND ASCENT 108

THE TURN 110

THE WILDERNESS ENDS 112

THE AUDACITY 114

GRACE 115

THE VERSION WORTH REMEMBERING 116

NOTHING LEFT TO PROVE 117

AND IT WAS GOD 118

ABOUT THE AUTHOR 121

THE KINGDOM OF ASH

I did not lose my inheritance when the fire came; I learned what could not burn.

HELL CAT

Something inside me shattered last night.
No sound.
Just a shift.
Like the settling of bones
after a break.

You didn't notice.
Most don't.
Not until it's already begun.

You wanted to see a hell cat.
And now she's pacing.
Silent.
Steady.
Smiling.

You've just unleashed her.
And she's not here to scream.
She's here to watch
what you love
decay.

If I were you—
I'd run.
But not because she's chasing.
She never does.

She waits.
And makes the ruin
come to her.

LOVE MADE A LIAR

They say home is where the heart is,
 but lately I'm not sure.
 Even the heart knows nothing anymore.

It beats, but only out of habit—
 a tired drum in an empty room,
 echoing promises it can't keep.

The walls once painted with laughter
 now peel in silence.
 Every photograph is a ghost,
 every memory a wound reopening.

I used to trust the heart,
 its pull, its certainty—
 but love has made a liar of it.
 Now it stumbles,
 bleeding in circles,
 chasing what can't be found.

If home was ever real,
 it vanished with you.
 And all that remains
 is a hollow chest
 pretending to be alive.

WHY DO YOU HATE ME SO?

"Devil, devil,
 why do you hate me so?"

I whispered it first as a child,
 when nightmares pressed on my chest
 and shadows stretched longer than the moonlight.
 I whispered it again as I grew,
 when rejection came dressed in familiar faces,
 when betrayal poured itself into my cup
 and called itself love.

The silence mocked me.
 For years, I heard no answer—
 only the grind of chains I could not see,
 only laughter curling through my mind
 like smoke that choked but never burned away.
 The question festered,
 a wound beneath the skin of my soul:
 why me? why always me?

I couldn't understand
 why I was always the target,
 why I was different,
 why the arrows seemed to find me
 even in crowds,
 why the fire burned hotter beneath my feet
 than under anyone else's.
 "I've done nothing to deserve this," I cried,
 "nothing to warrant the storm."

I carried it through deserts where prayers dried on my tongue,
through valleys where graves called my name.
I carried it through nights of blood on my pillow,
through mornings that tasted like iron.
Still, no voice came—
only war in unseen places,
only storms that tore without warning,
only silence
thick enough to drown in.

But one day,
when the battle left me sprawled in the dust,
when my fists were bloodied
from swinging at shadows,
the silence broke.
Not with thunder,
not with trumpet or flame,
but with a voice slick as oil,
a *hiss* that slithered across my spine,
coiling tighter with every word.

Finally, the devil responded.

"*I hate you,*" he seethed,
"*because you wear a crown I can never touch.*
I hate you because even in your weakness
He calls you His.
I hate you because His blood bought you,
and no scheme of mine can unwrite that purchase.

I hate you because your worship
reminds me of the throne I craved
but could never claim.
I hate you because you were chosen,
and I was cast down.

Your rising is my ruin.
Your existence, my torment.
Every scar you carry becomes a testimony,
and every time you fall yet stand again,
Heaven sings—
and I cannot bear the sound.

I hate you because when you stumble,
angels rush to your side.
Because when you whisper His name,
I feel the chains around me rattle.
Because your prayers
are hammers that crack my skull.
I hate you because the light in you
is the very flame that scorches me.

I hate you because you are chosen,
because you are loved,
because you are marked as His own.
And I—
I will never escape the chains I forged for myself.
So I hurl mine at you,
hoping you'll drown in the pit I dug,
hoping you'll forget who you are.

But even when I roar,
even when I strike,
you bear His name like fire on your forehead.
And that name—
that Name above every name—
is the very sword that slays me."

The words struck me deeper than any blade.
For the first time, I understood:
his fury was not my curse,
but my confirmation.
The hatred was not proof of my weakness,
but proof of my belonging.

And there, with hell itself confessing its jealousy,
I wept—
not from fear,
but from the holy weight of knowing.

I am hated,
because I belong to Jesus.
I am despised,
because I am a child of God.

And suddenly the chains rattled loose,
the shadows shrank back,
and the silence became a song.
For I realized—
if the devil hates me this much,
then Christ must love me
beyond measure.

WHY DO I CHASE YOU?

Why do I chase you
if I know I cannot win?
I was meant to be the prize,
the one who stood still while others
fought for a glimpse of my gaze.

But somewhere between your silence
and my yearning,
I became the beggar,
stretching out hands that once held
the power to choose.

You were supposed to call my name,
to feel your chest tighten with the fear
of losing me.
Instead, I am the one out of breath,
running after shadows
that never stop long enough
to look back.

And yet—
something in me whispers
that if I run far enough,
if I endure the sting of being unseen,
you'll remember
what it feels like to be the one
in pursuit.

But maybe that's the lie I tell myself,
the trap I willingly enter,
because deep down I know:
chasing you is not the same as finding love.

One day, my feet will stop.
My lungs will refuse to burn for you.
And when they do—
you will remember the taste of hunger,
the sharp ache of thirst.

You'll crawl toward me
with the desperation I once carried.
But I will not turn.
I will not wait.
I will let you starve on the silence
you once fed me.

DON'T BE SO FAMILIAR WITH HEARTBREAK

Don't be so familiar with heartbreak
that you know the rhythm by heart—
like second nature,
like breathing in the ache before it starts.
Like bracing for thunder
even when the sky is clear.

Don't let grief become a groove
you fall into with closed eyes,
calling it comfort
when it's just repetition in disguise.

You were not born to cradle sorrow
like a hymn passed down through bloodlines,
not meant to hum pain
like a lullaby learned too young.
Not every ache is inheritance.
Not every silence is sacred.

There's a difference between surviving
and surrendering.
Between naming your wounds
and letting them write your name.

Don't rehearse sadness
just because joy feels unfamiliar.

Don't run back to ruins
just because they remember your name.

You deserve a love
that doesn't require you to shrink.
A peace that doesn't echo
the footsteps of those who left.
A tenderness that teaches you
new rhythms—
not ones that bleed,
but ones that bless.

So when heartbreak knocks again,
don't answer like a host.
Don't set a table for sorrow.
Don't memorize the music of mourning
like it's the only song your soul can sing.

Instead,
listen for the sound
of your own healing.

It's quieter—
but it's there.
And it's yours.

THE SAME WORDS

The same words that cradle you in the night,
Soft whispers of comfort, tender, light,
Will rise as swords in the shadowed dawn,
Judging the path your soul has drawn.

Truth does not falter, though hearts may stray,
What soothes today may demand to weigh.
Grace offered freely, yet justice stands near,
A mirror reflecting what you hold dear.

So tread with care on this fleeting plane,
For words that heal can also reign.
Both balm and burden, they mark your place,
The measure of love, the shadow of grace.

THE PAST

"Forgive and forget."
A tidy little phrase.
Convenient for the ones who never paid.

But how do you forget
when their patterns resurrect the past
with every careless word,
every familiar silence?

They ask you not to bring it up again.
And you agree—
not because you've healed,
but because you've learned:
some people don't want reconciliation.
They want amnesty.

They promise to change,
but their words are as empty
as the actions that follow them.
Their apologies echo—
loud, rehearsed, and hollow—
always spoken in future tense,
never lived in the present.

Everything you name,
they label a lie.
And when they run out of excuses,
they reach for God—
using His name to whitewash their wrongs,

to paint their guilt in holy tones.
But God is not mocked.
He sees what's done in secret.
He knows the difference
between repentance
and manipulation.

It was never about forgiveness.
Never about letting go.
It was about permission—
permission to repeat,
to rewrite,
to recast your pain as pettiness.

They made a home out of your silence,
set the table with denial,
and called it peace.

But you know better now.
You see the choreography—
the way they twist memory into manipulation,
remorse into performance.

They never wanted to be free *with* you.
They wanted to be free *from* accountability.

And so you stop trying to forget.
You stop trying to fold your truth
into a version that makes them comfortable.

You remember—
  not to hold a grudge,
  but to hold a boundary.

Because this time,
  you choose clarity over closeness.
  Still. Quiet. Unshaken.
  And fully awake.

TOO MUCH FOR YOU TO SWALLOW

I was never meant to be consumed easily.

I came with questions you didn't want to answer,
 depth you didn't plan to wade through,
 truth that refused to sweeten itself
 just to be palatable.

You wanted me diluted—
 small sips,
 bite-sized honesty,
 a woman you could admire
 without having to change.

But I arrived whole.

Unapologetic in my becoming.
 Uncomfortable in my clarity.
 Too loud in rooms that thrived on silence,
 too discerning for hands that only knew how to take.

You mistook my fullness for arrogance,
 my boundaries for bitterness,
 my discernment for disobedience.

But I was never difficult—
 I was intact.

I asked you to rise.
 You asked me to shrink.

So you called me "too much,"
 as if excess was my crime
 instead of your appetite being small.

Understand this—
 I was not meant to go down easy.

I was meant to choke
 every lie you told yourself
 about what you were capable of holding.

And if loving me
 felt like something stuck in your throat,
 it's because truth has a way
 of refusing to be swallowed whole
 by those who fear being transformed.

SIMMERING

Simmering,
 like a pot about to boil over—
 not quite yet,
 but you can hear it whisper,
 you can see the steam rising.

The blessings of God
 are not fast food,
 not thrown together in haste.
 They are marinated,
 seasoned with eternity,
 left on low fire
 so every drop of flavor seeps deep.

You call it waiting,
 but heaven calls it preparation.
 You say delay,
 but God says design.

For when you simmer,
 you are being softened,
 all the hardness breaking down
 until what comes forth
 is tender,
 ready,
 perfected for the table of destiny.

Simmering means the promise
 isn't absent—

it's in process.
The fragrance rises before you see the feast,
and every moment teaches your spirit:
slow does not mean denied,
for the vision is yet for an appointed time,
though it linger, it will not delay.

So change your language.
Don't say, "I am waiting."
Say, "I am simmering."
Because what He is crafting in you
is too holy to be rushed,
too weighty to be half-done.

And when the lid finally lifts—
child, you will see it:
abundance bubbling over,
favor spilling out,
blessing poured so richly
that the plowman overtakes the reaper
and the memory of famine disappears.

What God simmered in secret
will be unveiled in glory.
You will not just taste,
you will be filled,
for the Lord is good,
and out of your belly
rivers of living water will flow.

Not early.
Not late.
But right on time—
the time chosen before the foundations of the earth,
when He makes everything beautiful in its season.

And then you will know:
the simmer was never silence.
It was heaven working unseen,
breathing fire beneath your promise,
cooking your destiny
to perfection.

LET THE BRIDGES BURN

I've reached the place where the smoke rises behind me,
 bridges burning I once swore I'd never set aflame.
 I've cut loose hands I thought would always hold mine,
 not because I've "leveled up,"
 but because I've grown.

Growth teaches you to unclench.
 To let go.
 To stop confusing history with destiny.
 Not everyone who walked with you yesterday
 is qualified to stand beside you tomorrow.
 Some were sent only for a season,
 and when that season ends,
 you must know how to release—
 before their presence becomes dead weight,
 before their silence becomes shackles,
 before their love turns into leeches
 sucking the breath from your chest
 when you were meant to breathe freely and rise.

I no longer set myself on fire
 just to keep others warm.
 I am no one's sacrifice.
 I've learned my worth is not found in what I give away,
 but in what I refuse to surrender.

And now I see it clear:
 Not every "friend" is truly for you.

Some smile while they sip from your soul.
Some clap only when you're standing still.
Some carry knives sharper than their words—
and they hide them in their laughter.

But friendship is not measured in years.
Sometimes the one you meet in passing
will pray harder for your blessing
than the one who's known you half your life.
Loyalty is not time.
Loyalty is truth.
And truth exposes the counterfeit.

So I sharpen my discernment,
I guard my circle like a crown,
I protect my peace like it is sacred—
because it is.

Let the bridges burn.
Let the ashes scatter.
Let the false ones fall away.

I am rising—
and those who cannot rise with me
were never meant to go where I'm going.

ACCESS REVOKED

I don't beg for scraps.

I know how crumbs are offered—
 slowly, deliberately,
 not to nourish
 but to keep me manageable.

God prepared me a feast.
 That knowledge cured me
 of confusing control
 with generosity.

I don't linger where dignity is rationed.
 I don't explain my worth.

Keep what you were willing to give.

Access revoked.

THE LOUDEST SILENCE

I learned that heaven can be quiet without being absent, and still demand everything of me.

FROM EGYPT TO MANNA

God had to move me—
 drag my trembling hands from Egypt's table,
 where leeks and onions numbed my hunger,
 and chains disguised themselves as comfort.

I cried for freedom,
 yet when the door split open,
 I almost mourned the taste of bondage.
 Slavery had rhythm,
 predictable rations of despair.

But manna does not fall in Egypt.
 It waits in the wilderness,
 where thirst cracks your lips
 and faith is your only compass.
 It waits where there is no map but trust,
 no guarantee but God's breath.

Manna descends like mercy,
 fresh every morning,
 unearned, unbought, undeniable.
 It silences Egypt's memory—
 this bread of heaven,
 this portion of promise,
 this taste of tomorrow.

So do not curse the wilderness.
 It is the threshold of provision.

The desert is where God proves Himself enough.
And if you're still starving,
it may be because you refuse to leave
the table of Pharaoh.

Better to be famished in the desert with God,
than full in Egypt without Him.

OFF THE MAP

I begged You for a roadmap.
I wanted the highway—
smooth, lit, predictable.
I wanted the destination
before the first step.

But You do not work
for my comfort.
And You do not negotiate
with my fear.

So You drove me into the dark.
Past the city limits
of my control.
Past the borders
of my five-year plan.

I screamed that we were lost.
Pointed at exit signs we missed.
Clawed at the door handle,
desperate to return
to the safety I recognized.

But You kept driving.

You took me to the edge of the map
because You knew
I would never find myself
on a paved road.

You didn't lead me
into the wilderness

to kill me.
You took me off-road
to prove
I could survive
without streetlights.

I don't know where we're going anymore.
And for the first time—
I don't care.

I am done trusting the map.
I am trusting the Maker.

I am no longer following a route.
I am following
the Shepherd.

UNBILLED JOURNEYS

I've had to return invoices for debts I didn't owe—
   bills addressed to my name, yet signed by someone else's hand.
   It taught me that not every burden belongs to me.
   Some weights are assignments disguised as obligations.

There are journeys you must take alone.
   Not because you're unloved,
   but because divine revelation requires privacy.
   There are seasons when explanations fail—
   when you cannot make sense of what God is doing,
   not to others,
   and not even to yourself.

But one day, the path will make sense in reverse.
   Every unanswered question will trace back to His intention.
   For now, you just walk, unpaid and unpraised,
   trusting that Heaven keeps better records than men.

NOT ON THE GUEST LIST

I am done checking for my name
on lists written by human hands.

I don't need a seat at tables
where I have to audition to eat.
I don't need to contort myself
to fit inside circles
designed to keep me out.

Keep your VIP access.
Keep your velvet ropes.

I am known by the King.
I carry the keys to the House.

And when you live in the Palace,
you don't wait in line—
you just go home.

TIGHT SCHEDULE

"You're young," they say—
as if youth can drown this hunger.

"You have time."
Not in my book.
Time is a thief,
slipping through cracks while my chest keeps its own clock.

"Don't rush."
I'm not rushing.
I'm on a deadline carved into my bones.

"There's plenty of fish in the sea."
Not for me.
The ocean is vast, but I was forged for one—
one flame, one match, one name.

"When the time is right, it will happen.
Not because they said it—
but because God already decreed it."

Still—
I ache for a man whose fire bends to no one but me.
Not a borrowed ember, not a passing flicker,
but a blaze that bows to no rival.

I am not too young.
I know what I want.
I was forged different—

iron in the age of clay.
That is not pride. It is truth.

But even iron rusts.
Even steel grows weary.
And I long for arms strong enough
to carry the weight I cannot name aloud.

I want my life partner.
My soulmate.
My twin flame.

And when we ignite,
let the world see the blaze—
a fire struck in heaven,
untouchable, unending.

WHEN WE ARE DOWN TO NOTHING

When hands are empty,
 and prayers fall like whispers
 against the ceiling of silence,
 when strength has packed its bags
 and tomorrow looks like famine—
 God is up to something.

When doors slam shut,
 and the road crumbles beneath your feet,
 when the wilderness feels endless
 and even your tears feel wasted—
 God is up to something.

For He is the God who parts seas
 when the army is pressing near,
 the God who rains manna
 when the cupboards are bare,
 the God who raises bones from dust
 and hope from ashes.

So when you are down to nothing,
 don't lose your breath—
 take a deeper one.
 Because the grave was empty,
 the stone was rolled,
 and the throne is still occupied.

Your nothing is not the end.
 It's the breeding ground of miracles.

And when God is up to something—
everything changes.

ETCHED IN SILENCE

I may not bear tattoos that the world admires,
 but pain and betrayal have pressed their ink upon me.
 Lines invisible to the eye,
 yet etched deeper than any needle could carve.

These designs are not chosen,
 but they remain—
 delicate reminders of what was lost,
 and who I became because of it.

Each scar whispers a story
 I never asked to live through.
 Each mark carries a weight
 I never sought to carry.
 And still—
 they rest upon me like a second skin,
 a testament to both breaking and endurance.

My ink is not loud,
 yet it speaks.
 It reminds me that even wounds
 can hold wisdom.
 That survival itself
 is a kind of beauty,
 etched softly,
 but never erased.

I WISH I COULD TELL YOU

When you ask me my name,
 I part my lips, but the syllables falter—
 like something foreign, something borrowed,
 never quite belonging to the shape of my mouth.

I know the name I was given,
 the one inked on paper, stitched into memories,
 spoken with certainty by those who claim to know me.
 But when I utter it myself, it drifts—
 a specter of identity that never fully settles in my chest.

Most days, I feel like a witness to my own existence,
 watching from the periphery as my body moves
 through rehearsed routines, practiced smiles,
 a life that fits but never quite feels like my own.

I press my palm to the glass, searching for recognition,
 but my reflection stares back like a half-finished thought.
 A whisper of something I should know—
 but don't.

Maybe that's why my name hesitates on my tongue,
 why I stall in the silence between question and answer,
 afraid that to claim it is to claim a self
 I have yet to truly meet.

Everyone else seems certain of me—
 as if they've read a book I've yet to open.

And so I let them write me into being,
while I remain lost in the margins.

So when you ask my name,
I wish I could tell you.
But all I have is the pause,
and the quiet ache of not knowing.

DON'T LET GO

I almost let go.

Not loudly.
Not in rebellion.
Quietly—
the way people stop believing without announcing it.

I still prayed.
Still said "amen."
Still showed up looking faithful.

But inside,
I was tired of being strong for a God
who kept asking me to wait.

I was tired of hoping responsibly.
Tired of explaining away silence.
Tired of watching doors open for everyone else
while mine stayed closed
like I'd missed some invisible requirement.

I didn't stop believing in God—
I stopped believing He was going to choose me.

I wondered if my faith was too small
or my timing too late
or if I was simply... overlooked.

I asked questions I never planned to ask.
The kind you whisper into pillows
because you're afraid heaven might hear them wrong.

Did I mishear You?
Did I imagine the promise?
Was the waiting the point—or the punishment?

I was angry.
Then ashamed for being angry.
Then exhausted from pretending I wasn't either.

I stood close to the edge—
not of unbelief,
but of surrender.

And that scared me more than doubt ever did.

Because even at my weakest,
I still wanted God.

Even when faith felt humiliating.
Even when hope felt foolish.
Even when trust felt like self-betrayal.

I didn't let go
because something in me refused to believe
that the God who carried me this far
would abandon me in the middle.

So I stayed.

Not confident.
Not brave.
Just present.

And that—
that was enough to keep me alive
until faith could find me again.

I DIDN'T FORCE HEAVEN

I don't wanna bend Your will until it breaks,
 or press my prayers so hard
 that they become demands.

I've learned that sometimes my tears
 sound too much like begging,
 and my faith, too much like fear
 dressed up as devotion.

You are not clay for my shaping.
 You are the Potter—
 and I, the trembling vessel
 still learning to stay on the wheel.

So teach me the rhythm of surrender,
 how to kneel without resistance,
 how to want without control.

Because even when I don't understand,
 I know Your no is still mercy,
 and Your silence is not absence—
 it's just another way of saying,
 wait.

IT'S ALREADY LATE

Don't wait for the perfect timing—
it's already late.
The stars won't align
until you start walking toward them.

You've prayed for a sign,
but the answer was in your pulse—
steady, waiting,
tired of your hesitation.

The clock is jealous
of the purpose you keep postponing.
The door you've been staring at
was never locked,
just waiting for you to turn the handle.

Stop rehearsing the courage
you already have.
The world won't pause
until you feel ready—
so go, even trembling.
Go, before destiny
finds someone else
who moved.

TIME IS TICKING

When silence is your only answer.
You've buried hope
and called it closure,
labeled the grave
with prayers that never got a reply.

It's been four days.
Too late for healing.
Too early to forget.
The stone is rolled,
the crowd is gone,
and even your faith
smells like death.

You're folding.
Hands trembling over a white flag,
ready to hand your heart to the dark—
because what kind of God shows up
after the funeral?

But then—
He does.

Not in haste.
Not in guilt.
Just steady,
like time bends to meet Him.

"Where did you lay it?"
He asks—
not because He doesn't know,
but because you need to remember
where you stopped believing.

You flinch.
"It stinks."
And so does your disappointment.

But He doesn't scold.
He only smirks—
like He's seen the ending
and the ending is written:
death doesn't win.

Then He calls it:
"Come forth."

And suddenly,
what you mourned
starts moving.

No war.
No weeping.
Just resurrection
with a whisper.

"It was only sleeping,"
He says,
like it was never in question.

You called it over.
 He called it an intermission.
 You counted the days.
 He counted the glory.

Four days late,
 by your clock.
 Right on cue,
 by His.

THE HOLY INTRUSION

God did not ask if I was ready—He spoke because the time had come.

WHEN I KNEEL

I kneel before my God
 so that I can stand before any man,
Because to know Him
 is to know how it all began.

God alone can promote—
 He's the antidote,
The dose that kills my ego
 but revives my hope.

The architect of silence,
 He builds me in stillness,
Chisels purpose from pain
 and names me in hiddenness.
They saw me breaking—
 He saw me becoming.
While I wept through the night,
 He was oiling my running.

He is the pulse in my pause,
 The sigh between my scriptures,
The ink in my tears
 when I ran out of pictures.
They tried to write me off—
 He rewrote the scene.
I was the lost cause,
 He called: "redeemed."

Every "not yet" was heaven's poetry—
a love letter laced with wait.
A "no" in man's mouth
was just God changing the gate.

I don't bow for pity,
I bow for power.
Because mercy drips slow
in the midnight hour.
And what looks like groaning
is God ghostwriting glory—
Each breath a prophecy,
each bruise a backstory.

He hides me in the hollow of His voice
and lets me rest between verses.
When I was too weary to worship,
He translated my curses.

So let the world call it weakness
that I kneel this low—
But I've learned that deep roots
are how olive trees grow.

My posture is the prophecy.
My tears, intercession.
Even on my face,
I'm still a weapon.

Because when I kneel,
He stands.

And when I break,
He builds with His hands.

CONVERSATION AT THE ALTAR

Lord, do You hear me?
Because it feels like You've gone deaf to my prayers.
Every blessing I've begged for —
You've placed in someone else's hands.

> *I hear you. I have never stopped listening.*
> *The gifts I give to others do not cancel the ones I've stored for you.*
> *Your portion is still being prepared, and it will fit only you.*

But it feels cruel, Lord.
I clap at weddings while I walk home alone.
I smile at baby showers while my arms stay hollow.
Is this some lesson You're rubbing into my skin?

> *No, Beloved.*
> *I am not cruel.*
> *I am not mocking you.*
> *I am guarding you from loves that would wither*
> *and futures that would shatter.*
> *The ache you carry is proof of the room I've carved for joy to enter.*

Yet I've prayed more, waited longer,
held fast to purity while others ran free.
Why them? Why not me?

> *Because I am not building you for scraps.*
> *What you call delay is Me refusing to give you less than holy.*

Others may stumble into what looks like fullness,
but I am fashioning for you a covenant that will not break.

Still, I am tired, Lord.
This waiting feels like abandonment.

> *You are not abandoned.*
> *You are hidden — like seed pressed deep in the earth.*
> *The darkness you feel is not death but germination.*
> *And when the season turns,*
> *your life will burst open with the fruit of every prayer you ever*
> *prayed.*

So my emptiness is not the end?

> *No.*
> *Your emptiness is the space where I will pour abundance.*
> *Your story is not a footnote — it is a testimony in progress.*
> *And when you see what I've been shaping,*
> *you will not envy, you will not question.*
> *You will only say: Surely, the Lord was faithful.*

THE ALTAR I BUILT

I asked Him:
"Lord, the altar I built...
is it holy?
Is it one You accept?

Have I given You my best,
or am I bowing at the wrong fire?
Tell me, Father—
is this worship... or rebellion disguised as sacrifice?"

And His reply came—
a voice that shook my bones like thunder,
yet wrapped around me like a whisper of fire:

>*My child, listen to Me.*
>*The sacrifices you've been offering...*
>*they have not reached My throne.*
>*They were never Mine.*
>*You have lifted them up to gods that cannot see,*
>*cannot hear,*
>*cannot save.*

And suddenly I saw it—
how easy it is to drift.
Sometimes you get so caught up in the everyday movements
that you begin to exalt other things, other gods,
and neglect your Heavenly Father.
You don't even notice at first.
It doesn't happen all at once.

It's subtle.
One small compromise here, one distraction there—
until by the time you realize you've strayed,
you're already out in the deep end,
far from shore,
wondering how you got there.

I trembled, and asked:
"Then what must I do?
I thought I was serving You.
I thought these offerings pleased You."

Again His voice thundered—
shaking the walls of my heart,
cutting through every excuse,
every self-made altar:

> *Come back to your first love.*
> *Return to the flame I placed within you.*
> *Tear down the altars I never commanded you to build.*
> *Strip them to dust.*
> *For I am a jealous God.*
> *I do not share My glory with another.*
> *You must choose—Me, or them.*

His words burned.
Conviction pierced me deeper than any sword.
I saw every idol I had excused,
every compromise I had embraced,
every strange fire I had dared to place before Him.

So I answered, with tears:
"Then I will tear them down.
Every altar not built by Your hand,
I will crush to nothing.
I will rip away what I once called sacred,
because if You reject it, Lord—
I reject it too.

I love You too much to fail You now.
I promised You once that I would make it somehow,
and I will not break that vow.
Not now. Not ever."

And I did.
I tore it all down—
every idol, every compromise,
every place I thought was holy but was really profane.
I ripped it all to shreds.

Because to lose the mercy and grace of God
is too high a price.

And when the last altar fell,
when the noise of false gods died out,
I heard Him again.
This time not thunder,
but a whisper softer than breath:

    Welcome home.

WHEN I FINALLY SEE

Lord—
I see it now.
I've been kneeling at an altar I built from my own fears,
feeding it scraps of my faith
and calling it devotion.

Every doubt I nursed,
every moment I withheld my trust
was a quiet betrayal,
a slow turning of my back.
I thought I was waiting on You,
but I was worshiping my worry instead.

I traded the truth You spoke over me
for whispers from mortal mouths,
lowered what You lifted in me
just to feel a love that could not hold me.
I questioned my worth
while carrying the fingerprints
of the God who named me priceless.

I rushed ahead of You—
measuring life by clocks and deadlines
as if eternity bends to minutes.
I forgot heaven keeps its own time.

And now the weight of it hits me:
this isn't just wandering,
it's surrendering my birthright of peace.

Yet even here, in this realization,
You find me.
Mercy finds me.
You call me Your own
while I'm still on my knees
before an empty altar.

I cannot promise perfection,
only this breaking open,
this raw confession.
But let it be enough—
for if You still call me Yours,
then even in my ruins
I have found home.

THE SHAKING

Suddenly, there comes a time when there is a shaking.
What once felt certain begins to quake,
the ground beneath your feet trembles,
and the walls you leaned on no longer hold.

At first, it feels like loss.
Like the undoing of everything you trusted.
But the shaking does not come to bury you—
it comes to unearth you.

It rattles loose the dead weight,
tears away false securities,
and breaks the locks on doors
you never thought would open.

The very tremors that unsettle your world
are the same ones breaking the seal to your future.
The fractures become fault lines of glory,
and through them, light pours in.

For in the wake of the shaking,
a portal opens—
not to despair, but to blessing.
Not to ruin, but to promise.

And what felt like breaking
was only the sound of heaven
making room for your becoming.

WHEN THE KING CALLS

When the King calls,
 He does not whisper.
 He summons you by name,
 and your name reverberates
 like thunder through eternal halls.

Eyes may burn holes into your back,
 tongues may sharpen themselves in secret,
 but you walk forward, unshaken.
 Head high. Shoulders squared.
 For you are not approaching them—
 you are approaching Him.

The throne room yawns open.
 Silence thick as incense.
 The King is waiting.
 Seated. Eternal.
 Eyes fixed only on you.

One step.
 Two steps.
 Three.

You fall to your knees—
 the ground trembling beneath your weight.
 He lets the silence linger,
 measuring every beat of your heart.

Then His voice breaks the stillness:

"I have reviewed the books.
I have gone through the lists.
And you—
you are chosen to be blessed.

Not next in line.
Not tomorrow.
But now.

I have seen the tears you hid in the night.
I have counted every drop,
and I will repay.

It is your time."

Then He turns to the sneering crowd,
and His voice roars like fire on stone:

"You dared laugh at the one I love.
You plotted against the one I sealed.
You thought their silence meant I had forsaken them.
But I watched, and I wrote it down.

Now hear My decree:
the one you rejected, I have elevated.
The one you mocked, I have crowned.
Their rising will be your rebuke,
and their blessing will stand as your judgment.

Touch not what I have anointed.
For every sneer, I will return sevenfold honor.

For every stone you raised,
I will build them a throne."

And when the King speaks,
heaven records it,
hell trembles at it,
and the earth must bow beneath it.

WHERE LOGIC KNEELS

When God steps into the picture,
logic bows its head in silence.
For reason has no seat
in the council of the Divine.

He moves in ways the mind cannot map—
beyond blueprint, beyond comprehension—
for He is the Architect of calm—
and chaos still answers to His voice—
the Composer of patterns
too intricate for our finite sight.

Our logic trembles at His mysteries.
It cannot measure eternity,
cannot quantify grace,
cannot chart the coordinates of a miracle.

He is the Sovereign—
the rule beyond all rules,
the Law who wrote the laws of men
and breaks them as He pleases,
for even order answers to His voice.

We may never decipher Him—
how can dust decode Divinity?
How can the clay comprehend
the thoughts of the Potter's mind?

So let us not explain,
  but *exalt.*
Let us not define,
  but *deepen* in awe.

For to serve Him—
  the Ancient of Days,
  the Infinite clothed in light—
  is to stand barefoot on holy ground,
  and whisper, with trembling lips,
  "You are God, and that is enough."

THE ROD AND THE STAFF

The Lord is my shepherd—
so why do I run
as if I'm still being hunted?

You make me lie down
in green pastures,
yet I stand watch,
muscles locked,
convinced that rest is a snare.

You lead me beside still waters,
but I keep stirring the surface,
afraid of what might stare back at me
from the quiet.

Even when I walk through valleys
draped in shadow,
I forget the most unsettling truth
about the Shepherd:

You carry a rod.

Not to strike me—
but to shatter the jaw
of whatever thinks I am prey.

So I fear no evil,
not because it's absent,
but because You are
dangerous enough
to make it heel.

THE WEAPON

I begged You for the knife.

I pleaded for the sharp thing—
the shining thing,
the thing that dazzled
in everyone else's hands.

I am ready, I screamed.
I am strong enough to hold it.

But You stood in the doorway.
Silent.
Immovable.
A massive *No*
blocking out the sun.

I fought You for it.
Mistook Your protection
for pain.

I called it punishment.
I called it unfair.

I didn't know
that in my unhealed grip,
the blessing
would have become a blade.

I would have split myself open
trying to carry a weight
meant for a woman
fully grown.

You didn't withhold it to hurt me.
You withheld it
so I wouldn't bleed out
on the very gift
I asked You for.

WHO AM I TO CHANGE YOUR MIND

If you've already decided who I am,
 then wear your illusion proudly.
 I'm done auditioning for parts
 in stories I never agreed to star in.

You built a version of me from rumor and reach,
 then got mad when I refused to play her.
 You called it pride—
 I call it peace.

Maybe I was never meant to fit
 inside your fragile definition of enough.
 Maybe I was born to break the frame
 and make you question why you needed one.

If you've already decided who you want me to be,
 then keep your verdict.
 I'm not here to convince—
 I'm here to *exist*.

And when my silence echoes louder
 than all your assumptions combined,
 remember this:
 I never needed your understanding
 to be divine.

THE POTTER'S HANDS

I know now—
 the gifts I hold were never mine to keep.
 They were borrowed light,
 reflections of the One who kindled them in me.

For without the Master,
 I am but a lump of clay—
 silent, formless, forgotten dust
 waiting for breath to make me whole.

But when His hands press upon me,
 when He molds and shapes and smooths my edges,
 I begin to remember who I am—
 who I was always meant to be.

Each turn of His hand births purpose.
 Each stroke of His palm whispers grace.
 And I rise—
 not in my own strength,
 but in the rhythm of His creating.

Yet I must not forget—
 that beauty is borrowed,
 that glory is lent.
 The moment He removes His touch,
 I crumble back into what I was:
 shapeless, lifeless, undone.

So I hold His gifts with trembling hands,
knowing they are His to use,
His to take,
His to fill with light again.

For even to be called His own
is mercy I could never earn,
and breath I do not deserve.

HE KNOWS WHAT I CANNOT SEE

Time has taught me that God sees what I cannot.
He hears conversations I'll never know took place,
shields me from paths that would have drained my peace,
and closes doors that weren't built to hold my heart.

Those prayers I once wept over—
the ones I believed were the only answer,
the ones I thought I needed to survive—
I now praise Him for turning away.

Because every "no" was a shield with glory hidden inside.
Every detour was divine protection.
Every delay was a step toward destiny.
Some blessings arrive wrapped in disappointment,
and some miracles first appear as loss.

There were people I begged Him to keep in my life...
He removed them quietly.
There were opportunities I was desperate for...
He shut them firmly.
And it hurt.
But later—when truth rose to the surface—
His "no" revealed itself as mercy.
A rescue.
A bullet never allowed to reach me.

God's "no" is never rejection.
It is redirection.
It is the hand of a Father who refuses to let my future bleed.

It is the whisper:
"Daughter, I'm saving you for better."

So now I walk slower.
I pray with open hands.
I trust the doors He closes as much as the ones He opens.
Because His silence is still protection.
His detours are still love.
And His "no" is still a promise—
that His plans for me run deeper and kinder
than anything I could ever imagine.

I rest in that.
I trust in that.
I thank Him even when I don't understand—
because I know one day I will look back
and see that every "no" was God's way of saying,
"I love you too much to let you settle."

THE SABOTAGE

I built a life
with my own two hands.
Laid the foundation.
Locked the doors.
Set the table
for a future I chose.

And then—
You burned it down.

You didn't send a warning.
You sent a match.

I watched the smoke rise,
choking on the ashes
of my five-year plan,
screaming at the sky,
Why would You ruin me?

But when the smoke cleared,
I saw what was hiding
beneath the floorboards
of the house I built:

Rot.
Traps.
Dead ends.

You didn't ruin my life.
You sabotaged
my destruction.

You loved me too much
to let me succeed
at the wrong thing.

GOD KEEPS RECORDS

God keeps records —
  not of perfection,
  but of persistence.
  Of the nights you whispered *"help me"*
  when no one else heard.
  Of the tears that baptized your pillow
  when you thought Heaven was silent.

He remembers the prayers you buried,
  the ones you stopped saying out loud.
  He kept them —
  every syllable, every sigh,
  folded neatly between His promises.

And when your story reaches the page
  marked *"impossible,"*
  He smiles.
  Because that's where His signature belongs —
  inked in mercy, sealed in grace,
  stamped with the words:
  "It is finished."

NOT LIKE MAN

God Is Not Like Man
It's something I've come to understand—
not in a moment,
but slowly,
like light rising in a room I didn't know was dark.

He doesn't keep score.
He doesn't withdraw His love when we fail.
He forgives—
not reluctantly,
but freely,
again and again.

God is not naïve.
But He is kind.

God is not like man.
He doesn't sway with moods
or shift with time.
He is steady—
an anchor when the tide pulls everything else away.

He doesn't turn His face when we're at our worst.
He draws near.
Not to shame us,
but to wash us clean,
to call us His.

God is not like man.
When others forget,
He remembers.
When they leave,
He stays.
Silently holding what we thought was too broken to carry.

He fulfills every promise—
not just the ones we cling to,
but even the ones we forgot we prayed.
And somehow,
He always gives more.

God is not like man.
And thank God—
because we need a love
that doesn't fail like ours does.
We need *Him*—
perfect,
where we are not.

THE KEEPER OF THE KEYS

God did not knock.
 He interrupted.

You were kneeling at the door,
 forehead pressed to the grain,
 reciting promises like passwords,
 hoping the lock would mistake effort for authority.

You called it faith.
 He called it fixation.

The door did not ask for your devotion—
 you gave it anyway.
 Fastened your hope to hinges,
 mistook access for approval,
 and dressed anticipation up as obedience.

Then Heaven stepped in
 and shifted the room.

Stop, He said—
 not cruelly,
 not loudly,
 but with the weight of truth that halts a soul mid-stride.

The door is not holy.
 It never was.
 It has no breath, no discernment, no mercy.
 It opens for thieves and kings alike.

You were never meant to trust wood and iron.
You were meant to trust
the hands that forged the key.

You made the promise an altar
and forgot the Promiser.
You worshipped *what could be*
and neglected *Who is.*

That is when pain entered—
not as punishment,
but as intrusion.

Pain disrupted your rhythm,
broke your grip on outcomes,
forced your hands open
when you refused to unclench them yourself.

Pain is the seed of purpose.
It is grace breaking ground,
love refusing to let you root
in what would eventually ruin you.

The delay was mercy.
The silence was protection.
The locked door was restraint.

And the One who holds the keys—
He never left.
He was watching to see
if you would release the door
before He trusted you with what lay beyond it.

Because some doors don't open
until worship is reordered.

And some blessings don't arrive
until God Himself
becomes the focus again.

THE PROLIFIC SUSPENSE WRITER

God is the most prolific suspense writer—
He lets the tension sit
like smoke in your lungs,
refusing to exhale
until your knees hit the floor.

He is not rushed
by your clock,
your threats,
your hunger.

He writes in silence,
in shutdowns,
in the echo of "Why me?"
that never gets an answer
until it's too late to matter.

He'll let the curtain close
and your faith unravel,
just to enter—
unannounced,
unapologetic,
unmistakable.

He kills the light,
waits until your voice cracks,
then whispers a line
that rewrites everything.

And that's the twist—
You thought He'd abandoned the story.
But He was building the tension
so your deliverance
wouldn't just be heard—
it would thunder.

THE HEAVY CROWN

Grace did not arrive to comfort me, but to place weight on my head and call it glory.

WHEN GOD ARISES

They wait in shadows,
 smiles sharp as blades,
 whispers curling like smoke in the night—
 "Surely the Lord was never with her,
 surely she will break."

Their laughter rises,
 but so does my God.

I hear their voices in the spirit,
 nets stretched across my path,
 pits carved for my fall—
 but the hand of the Almighty
 reaches further than their schemes,
 and what was meant to bury me
 becomes the soil for my rising.

I have known betrayal by familiar hands,
 false witnesses weaving lies
 from threads I never spun.
 Yet still I stand,
 not because I am unshaken,
 but because He is unshakable.

Let them scatter like ashes in the wind.
 Let their venom turn back on their tongues.
 For the Lord, my Defender,
 does not sleep,

does not slumber,
does not forget.

And when He comes—
not a moment late,
not a promise void—
He will silence their laughter,
rewrite my waiting into wonder,
and prove to the doubters
that faith is never wasted.

For God is within her,
she will not fall.
He upholds her at the break of day,
and carries her through the night.

He will put me back together
in front of those
who tried to break me apart.

So laugh if you must,
but mark this moment:
The pit you dug for me
is the grave you'll meet yourself in.

ROUSE THE ANCIENT OF DAYS

Let me speak plainly.
Are You still *that* God?
Not the tame one they preach about—
I mean *the God of old*,
the terror wrapped in smoke and flame,
who made empires crumble with a sigh.
The One whose breath split oceans.
Whose silence shook mountains.
Whose name alone made demons beg for pigs.

Because right now—
You feel absent.
You feel still.
You feel... *civilized.*

And I'm drowning.
Lied on.
Dragged through the dirt by hands You could break without blinking—
but don't.

They twist my name.
Turn truth into a weapon and laughter into a knife.
And You watch.

You. Watch.

But deep inside me,
beneath the bruises and disbelief,
something stirs.

A whisper.
A memory.
A madness.
That You *are still Him*.
Not gone. Not soft. Just waiting.
Like lightning behind locked lips.

You're not restrained—
You're *restraining Yourself.*
Power leashed by will.
Mercy gripping wrath by the throat.

But even mercy gets tired.
And when it does,
God doesn't walk in—
He *erupts.*

So rise, Ancient of Days.
Not as comfort—
as consequence.
Not as lamb—
as *lion with blood on His breath.*

Don't knock.
Break down the door.
Tear the heavens like curtains.
Make the earth remember fear.
Let every demon regret the morning they rose.
Let every lie fracture under the weight of truth sharpened in Your mouth.

Crush what hunts me.
Burn what follows me.
Let hell taste the edge of heaven's sword.
Let every shadow know this:

You don't touch what belongs to God and walk away whole.

And when You're done—
don't heal the wreckage.
Write Your name in it.

Let history remember:
God rose.
God roared.
And God *ravaged*.

THE OVERFLOWING SEASON

Eyes have not seen,
 ears have not heard,
 nor has the heart conceived
 the weight of glory about to break over you.

The storehouses of heaven creak with fullness.
 Angels lean over the balconies of eternity,
 whispering of your name,
 watching as God unseals the ledger of your faith.

Every seed you pressed into the soil of prayer,
 every sacrifice hidden from man's applause,
 is rising now—
 like wheat kissed by rain,
 like vineyards swelling with new wine,
 like oil breaking forth from the pressed olive.

Harvest has come.
 The plowman overtakes the reaper.
 The sower is met by the one bearing sheaves.
 What was buried in hope
 returns as rivers of abundance,
 flooding fields you thought were barren.

Prepare your vessels.
 Empty jars will not suffice.
 For the Lord of the Harvest has spoken:
 "I remember.

I have seen.
I repay."

Your barns will groan with overflow.
Your baskets will drip with honey.
Your cup will spill over its brim,
and nations will witness the proof of His covenant.

This is not delay.
This is not denial.
This is divine timing breaking open.
God Himself rises to demonstrate His faithfulness.
The Keeper of time is proving Himself true.

Lift your eyes—
for the clouds heavy with promise
are about to break over you.
Rain is coming.
Glory is coming.
And nothing can stop the season of your return.

DRIPPING IN FAVOR

As for me,
I don't beg for God's favor—
I demand it.
I want it pouring, flooding,
dripping so thick
they drown in the overflow.

When they see me,
let their throats tighten.
Let them choke on the evidence
that I am chosen—
not in empty titles,
but in the fire of every step I take.

They crowned themselves enemies,
just as Saul did with David—
but like David,
I will bury their slander
beneath the throne
they swore I'd never touch.

Let my name cut their gossip wide open.
Let it scorch their tongues raw.
Too sacred to shout,
too dangerous to spit loud—
for the moment they do,
I appear,
uninvited, unstoppable,
wearing the freedom they can't steal.

Favor is my vengeance.
Oil is my weapon.
God Himself cloaks me in a glory
that breaks their schemes
before their hands can move.

And here's the venom they can't escape:
they will watch.
Watch me rise,
while their curses collapse.
Watch me shine,
while their plots decay.
Watch me inherit,
while their hands stay empty.

They cannot touch what God has sealed.
And that truth will eat them alive.

NO CO-SIGNERS

God didn't authorize any co-signers
 on the promise He gave you.
 Your covenant is not up for auction,
 your destiny is not a group project.

He etched it in fire,
 sealed it with blood,
 and posted His Spirit
 as witness and guard.

So let them gather,
 let them whisper,
 let them draft their counterfeits in secret ink—
 every false contract burns
 when heaven breathes.

Stop begging for their signatures;
 their pens are brittle twigs,
 their names carry no weight.
 The deal was struck in eternity
 before they even learned to speak.

And when He calls you chosen,
 no courtroom in hell
 can overrule His decree.
 When He opens a door,
 no demon, no rival, no friend-turned-foe
 can weld it shut.

So walk like a storm,
  head high, feet steady—
  the covenant is yours,
  the inheritance secure.

God didn't authorize any co-signers.
  And if they dare press their names
  onto what He already sealed,
  may their ink dry in mid-air,
  may their signatures vanish like smoke,
  and may the weight of His Word
  crush every counterfeit beneath your feet.

DECREE OF THE TABLE

They raised their voices against me,
but Heaven heard every word.
They thought their poison was power,
their doubt a prison,
their laughter a grave.
But the Lord overturned their schemes.

This time it's personal.
The Shepherd Himself sets the table—
not in shadows,
but in the blinding fire of His glory.
He anoints my head with oil,
my cup spills over,
and the seat they coveted
is sealed with my name.

They will watch me feast
while famine eats their bones.
They will thirst
while my cup overflows.
They will choke
on the venom they spewed,
and their lies will return to their mouths
like dust and gall.

For this is the decree of the Lord:
Those who cursed you will be cursed.
Those who mocked you will bow.
And those who longed for your downfall

will waste away,
their teeth grinding only the ashes
of their own words.

THE MARK OF THE KING

You say you want to be used by God—
  but you still want the right to choose.
  You want His anointing
  without His authority.
  His glory
  without His government.
  His blessing
  without His breaking.

But hear me—
  God doesn't negotiate.
  He does not share His throne.
  He doesn't co-sign your dreams
  or rewrite His will to match your desires.
  He is the King.
  The Author.
  The Final Word.
  His promises stand: yes and amen.
  His covenant is blood-sealed,
  and His terms are not up for debate.

He sets the rules.
  He commands the steps.
  You either bow and follow,
  or you walk away empty.

And yet—
  what a weight,
  what a glory,

what an unspeakable privilege
to be chosen at all.
That the God of eternity
would press His seal upon mortal flesh,
and call your name in the courts of Heaven.

This is no casual thing.
No cheap crown.
No borrowed title.
This is the mark of the King.
It will cost you—
your pride, your comfort, your control.
But it gives you—
purpose, power, and a place in His story.

So don't wear His name like an accessory.
Don't carry His calling like it's optional.
This is covenant.
This is weight.
This is glory.

And if you bear the mark,
then walk like one set apart.
Speak like one branded by eternity.
Live like one honored with Heaven's trust.

For to be used by Him
is not a burden.
It is the highest honor.
The privilege of being a vessel
in the hands of the Almighty—

proof that the King Himself
has written your life into His plan.

UNTOUCHABLE IN GOD

Untouchable in God—
 that's where I am becoming.
 Not just hidden,
 but *enthroned* in His presence.
 Not just protected,
 but *possessed* by His peace.

I've buried myself in the folds of His robe,
 and the world can no longer trace my scent.
 Even hell's best trackers
 return empty-handed—
 because you can't hunt
 what's been sealed in glory.

I dwell where mortals lose their breath—
 in the cleft of the Rock,
 where His whisper splits mountains
 and His eyes ignite galaxies.
 There—
 that's where I rest.

My name is written in fire now,
 etched in the palms of the Ancient of Days.
 And when He covers me,
 no weapon remembers how to aim.

Let them summon storms.
 Let them sharpen words into swords.
 They'll find nothing but smoke and Shekinah,

because I am not here—
I'm *in Him.*

The shadow of the Almighty is my address.
The secret place is my inheritance.
I no longer walk—
I *abide.*

To be hidden in the Creator
is to be lost in light,
to move unseen through the dark,
to speak and watch walls crumble.

I am wrapped in eternity,
veiled in His breath,
fed by His fire.
And in that holy concealment,
I have become
unreachable.
Unshakable.
Untouchable.

ASHES AND ASCENT

I feel him near—
 closer than the hush between heartbeats,
 closer than tomorrow hiding inside today.

The veil thins.
 Revelation breathes.
 What was hidden will not stay buried;
 what was delayed will not be denied.

Every sorrow was a seed.
 Every tear watered the ground.
 Agony was not my ending—
 it was my anointing.
 Pain was prophecy in disguise,
 and now the promise ripens.

I do not see him with my eyes,
 but my soul knows his footsteps.
 The air shifts with his approach,
 the earth tilts toward our meeting.
 Destiny does not stumble—
 it arrives on schedule.

He is the tea to my cup—
 warmth filling emptiness.
 I am the rose to his garden—
 beauty rooting in his care.
 But together we are not simply flower and drink,
 we are fire and flame,

ashes and ascent.
A covenant combustion,
a blaze that heaven itself ordained.

When two become one,
let the world bear witness:
this union was written before time,
inked in eternity's ledger,
sealed by the hand of God.

And when I stand before him,
I will not ask,
I will not wonder.
I will speak the words creation
has been holding in its lungs—

Love has kept its promise.

THE TURN

I didn't wait for morning to break.
I broke the night myself.

No fanfare.
No golden rays.
Just the terrifying sound
of a woman
finished with waiting.

Yesterday,
I was asking for permission.
Today,
I issue decrees.

I'm done checking
the spiritual forecast.
I don't care if the wind is against me.
I don't care if the ground is hard.

I am not a victim of the season.
I am the force
that shifts it.

Favor is not
a gentle breeze on my face.
It is a weapon
in my hand—
the heavy, holy weight

of the King
backing every step I take.

So let the enemy brace himself.
I am not just walking
into my destiny.

I am hunting it down.

THE WILDERNESS ENDS

The wilderness ends
 not when the path clears,
 but when the lesson has done its work—
 when silence has shaped you,
 and storms have taught you how to stand.

When the ache becomes understanding,
 and the waiting no longer feels like punishment
 but preparation.

When you stop begging for the exit
 and start listening for the whisper,
 realizing the same voice that led you in
 is the same one that will lead you out.

The wilderness ends
 when the thirst for answers
 is replaced by the peace of surrender,
 and your heart learns to trust
 what your eyes still cannot see.

It ends when you look around
 and realize the desert has become a garden—
 not because the landscape changed,
 but because *you* did.

And in that stillness,
 when your soul finally exhales,
 you understand what the wilderness was for:

it was the altar where God met you—
to break you, to build you,
and to bring you home.

THE AUDACITY

They want me to mourn.
Watch me worship.

They want me to fold.
Watch me stand.

Hope is not a chirping bird.
It is a fist
raised against the dark.
It is the audacity
to stand in a graveyard
and demand to see the King.

It is staring at the dead thing
and refusing to bury it
because I know
the One
who breathes into dust.

Let them call me delusional.
I call it dangerous.

Because a woman who hopes
when all the lights go out—
she is the one thing
hell cannot figure out
how to kill.

GRACE

I did not become gentle
 by making myself smaller.
 I became gentle
 after surviving my own sharpness.

Grace is not silence.
 It is restraint.
 It is power that knows its reach
 and refuses to beg for permission.

I remain whole—
 undiluted, unmistakable.
 I no longer shrink to be digestible.
 I carry peace now
 because I am finished explaining myself.

If they choke,
 I wish them clarity
 and continue forward.

I am not less fire.
 I am fire refined—
 I know exactly
 when to warm,
 and when to burn.

THE VERSION WORTH REMEMBERING

There is a version of me worth remembering.
 Not because she was perfect,
 but because she was honest.

She was precious—naive, maybe even too trusting—
 yet she carried more than anyone realized.
 The world overlooked her,
 but she still pressed on with a quiet strength.

Remembering her keeps me from repeating the same cycles.
 She reminds me that endurance doesn't mean invisibility,
 and silence doesn't mean weakness.

That version of me whispered the truth:
 being last does not mean being unworthy.
 It does not mean forgotten.
 It means preserved.

They say they save the best for last.
 I say God saves the strongest for the end.
 Because in God's timing,
 last is often the beginning of something greater.

So I hold onto her,
 not to stay in the past,
 but to remember what she taught me:
 that time with God is never wasted.
 And His timing is never wrong.

NOTHING LEFT TO PROVE

I dragged the evidence in with bloody hands.
I cross-examined my own history,
screaming my defense at a jury of ghosts,
treating my survival like a plea bargain.
I wanted a verdict.
I wanted the world to admit
I bled enough to be here.

But the Judge wasn't looking at the evidence.
He was looking at the weapon in my hand.
He wasn't waiting for my closing argument.
He was waiting for me to stop fighting a case
He had already dismissed.
The gavel came down
before I ever took the stand.

So I am done auditioning for my own life.
Done screaming at a jury
that profits from my doubt.

I let the sword hit the floor.
I leave the files on the table.
The case is closed.
The record is sealed.

It is finished.

AND IT WAS GOD

I spent years suffocating in the sanctuary
of other people's expectations.
I wore their rules like heavy robes,
struggling to breathe beneath traditions
I never chose.

I memorized the script.
Performed the rituals.
Perfected the posture of holiness
while my soul starved in the pew.

I thought You lived inside the box they built.
I thought stepping outside the lines
meant losing You.

As the walls closed in,
I panicked.
I mistook the pressure for conviction.
I mistook the silence for absence.

So I stopped performing.
I loosened my grip.
I let the structure fall away.

I thought I was losing my faith.
I was only losing the cage.

Because out here—
without a script to recite,
without a role to maintain—
I finally noticed You—

El Roi,
the God who saw me
even when I couldn't see myself.
Immanuel,
the God who stayed
when everything familiar fell quiet.

You were not a list of demands.
Not a weight laid across my shoulders.
You were the breath filling my lungs
when I thought I was running out of air.

You were the strength in my jaw
when I refused to disappear.
The steady pulse beneath the noise
I had learned to call obedience.

I stop striving.
I exhale.

And I realize—
I never had to earn my way to You.
I only had to get quiet enough to feel
that You were with me
the whole time.

ABOUT THE AUTHOR

Ruth-Ann Walker writes for those who are discovering that breaking is not the end of the story, but often the beginning of something truer. Her work holds space for raw honesty and hard-won faith, tracing the quiet, often painful process of transformation.

She is the author of *Fragments of Grace* and now *Venom & Grace*, collections rooted in learning to recognize God in the silence and to trust Him in seasons that resist explanation.

She is usually writing, drinking coffee, or practicing the art of waiting—certain that Heaven does not need to be forced, only trusted.

www.ingramcontent.com/pod-product-compliance
Lightning Source LLC
Chambersburg PA
CBHW030547130626
46552CB00006B/2468